CONQUEROR WORM

HELLBOY

CONQUEROR WORM

by
MIKE MIGNOLA

Colored by
DAVE STEWART

Lettered by
PAT BROSSEAU

✠

Edited by
SCOTT ALLIE

Hellboy logo designed by
KEVIN NOWLAN

Collection designed by
MIKE MIGNOLA & CARY GRAZZINI

Published by
MIKE RICHARDSON

NEIL HANKERSON ✠ *executive vice president*

ANDY KARABATSOS ✠ *vice president of finance*

RANDY STRADLEY ✠ *vice president of publishing*

CHRIS WARNER ✠ *senior editor*

MICHAEL MARTENS ✠ *vice president of marketing*

ANITA NELSON ✠ *vice president of sales & licensing*

DAVID SCROGGY ✠ *vice president of product development*

MARK COX ✠ *art director*

DALE LaFOUNTAIN ✠ *vice president of information technology*

KIM HAINES ✠ *director of human resources*

DARLENE VOGEL ✠ *director of purchasing*

KEN LIZZI ✠ *general counsel*

Published by Dark Horse Comics, Inc.
10956 SE Main Street
Milwaukie, OR 97222

February 2002
First edition
ISBN: 1-56971-699-4

This book collects the four-issue series published by Dark Horse Comics.

1 3 5 7 9 10 8 6 4 2

PRINTED IN CANADA

MIKE MIGNOLA IS A GENIUS
An unapologetically subjective introduction

by GUILLERMO DEL TORO

Yes, Mike Mignola is a genius.

Right off the bat, we can agree on it. That's what makes writing an intro like this so easy. Especially if you were—like me—a groveling fan already. After all, Mike Mignola conjured up a perfect character in Hellboy, and his latest adventure, *Conqueror Worm*, is compelling and beautiful.

Nosiree, Bob. No problem: this introduction—like all of its kind—will merely point the reader to a few more reasons for grovelling at the feet of a comic-book demi-God like Mr. Mignola, here.

As a naïve young geek, I was fascinated by Mignola's legendary inking and penciling. I leafed through the art and drooled over the sensuous lines, bathed in those deep pools of blackness that appear in most every vignette Mike creates. And, like many heathens, I thought for a few issues that Hellboy was wearing goggles on his forehead. Then, at the end of *Wake the Devil*—when his horns sprout out—I realized what they were. I hurried back and actually re-read every story, searching out those issues that I was missing.

I was hooked. Or rather, I fell in love. Truly, madly, deeply in love.

As a matter of fact, my rediscovery of *Hellboy* is one of the happiest memories I have of shooting *Mimic* in Toronto. In spite of a grueling schedule, I often found myself waiting patiently for Silver Snail Comics to open. Once inside, I would browse through the bins hoping for a *Dark Horse Presents* issue that I somehow had missed. I loved reading a newly-found issue at 5:00 A.M. while my family slept and I prepared to storyboard that day's scenes.

I humbly confess that many a time I have aspired to imitate Mignola's mysterious style in the design of my films, especially the cold, velvet backdrop of darkness from which his characters emerge. Alas, his hyper-expressionistic lighting is—I've found out—almost impossible to reproduce in a 3-D world.

And then there are the moments of quiet, almost elegiac horror juxtaposed with a kinetic energy only hinted at by the best of Kirby. And then—and then—above all!—an irritating simplicity. A perfect, effortless line that reduces all us amateur illustrators to nothing but salivating Salieris prostrate before a Mozart symphony.

A few years ago, I had the pleasure of developing a *Hellboy* screenplay. I tried to honor and expand upon the universe created by Mike in his series and in his masterful short stories.

Mike's body of work is firmly anchored in the comic-book and literary traditions of Machen, Lovecraft, Toth, and Kirby. Yet what has been emerging from them is a species all its own.

In discussing the characters with Mike, I suggested that their fascinating, comforting immutability would need to yield to a more three-dimensional dramatic approach. In addition, a complete, self-contained screen drama would need to tie things up a bit more in the end.

I say this without a hint of criticism, for we work in parallel but separate arenas. In the illustrated stories, Mike finds a way to give us a calm, unfazed Hellboy, a quiet, always dignified Abe (my favorite character), or a tormented, almost biblical Rasputin.

And now … now … *Conqueror Worm* gives us something new, something more subtle and complete. We finally get an explanation of those Kirbyesque aliens in *Seed of Destruction*. At last, Hellboy lashes out at his benign captors at the BPRD. Lobster Johnson's origin and feats are expanded upon. In my fevered reading, all the characters seem more nuanced and evocative. Hell, even Roger the Homunculus becomes a brooding, almost Miltonian figure, conflicted by his origins and searching for an identity and purpose in life. Kriegaffe aside, the only character who remains delightfully one-dimensional is Lobster Johnson, and with a crazy-ass name like that, we shouldn't ask for more.

So, move in and explore these pages. They draw us into a deeper, richer universe; they crown all past work and signal a new promising future for the character, all while still giving us the pulp beauty, cheap thrills, and cosmic horrors that have become Mignola's signature.

A work of genius.

(Did I already mention that Mike Mignola is a genius?)

For Doc Savage, the Shadow,
the Spider, G-8, and the men who wrote them.
And for the original 11 1/2-inch G.I. Joe.

CHAPTER ONE

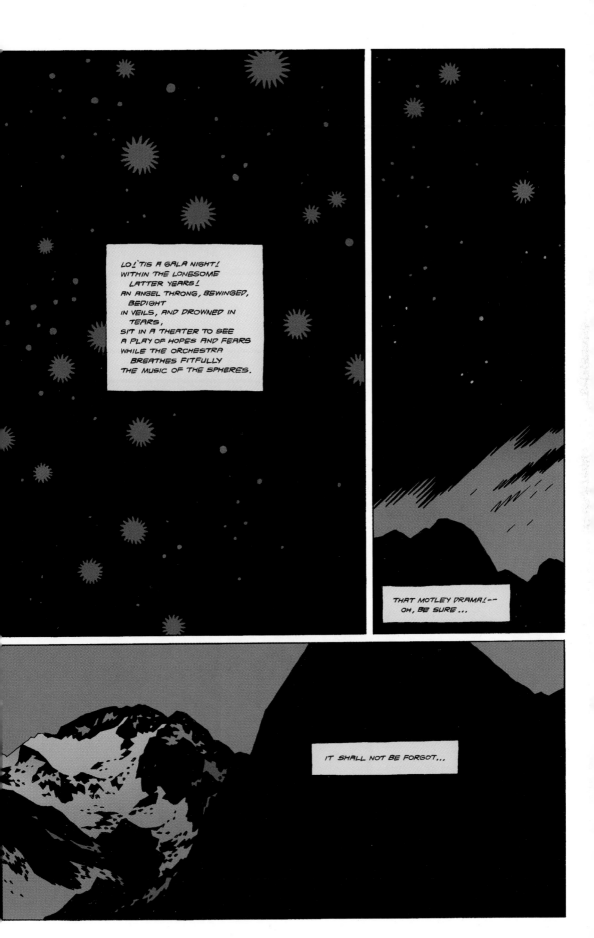

LO! 'TIS A GALA NIGHT!
WITHIN THE LONESOME
LATTER YEARS!
AN ANGEL THRONG, BEWINGED,
BEDIGHT
IN VEILS, AND DROWNED IN
TEARS,
SIT IN A THEATER TO SEE
A PLAY OF HOPES AND FEARS
WHILE THE ORCHESTRA
BREATHES FITFULLY
THE MUSIC OF THE SPHERES.

THAT MOTLEY DRAMA!--
OH, BE SURE...

IT SHALL NOT BE FORGOT...

OUT--OUT ARE ALL THE LIGHTS--OUT ALL! AND OVER EACH QUIVERING FORM:

THE CURTAIN, A FUNERAL PALL, COMES DOWN WITH THE RUSH OF A STORM...

AND THE ANGELS, ALL PALLID AND WAN, UPRISING, UNVEILING, AFFIRM...

THAT THE PLAY IS THE TRAGEDY, "MAN"...

AND ITS HERO THE CONQUEROR WORM.*

* FROM "LIGEIA" BY EDGAR ALLAN POE

"...BUT ON JANUARY 1, 1939, HE WAS ASSASSINATED, BLOWN UP IN HIS CAR ALONG WITH ALL HIS NOTES. THEN ...

"...SOMETHING STRANGE. THE GESTAPO MOVED WHAT WAS LEFT OF OEMING TO HUNTE CASTLE ...

"...ALONG WITH ASTRONOMERS, ASTROLOGERS, AND MYSTICS FROM ALL OVER EUROPE.

"OF COURSE, WE WEREN'T IN THE WAR YET, BUT THERE WERE PEOPLE IN WASHINGTON NERVOUS ABOUT WHAT *MIGHT* BE GOING ON UP THERE ...

"ON MARCH 20,* A FEW OF OUR TROOPS WENT IN TO 'INVESTIGATE,' AND THE TOP OF THE CASTLE BLEW OFF."

FIRE SPREAD THROUGH THE ENTIRE CASTLE, KILLING EVERYONE THERE.

I REMEMBER GUYS TALKING ABOUT THAT WHEN I WAS A KID. THAT WAS THE LAST LOBSTER JOHNSON MISSION.

LOBSTER WHO?

DON'T PAY ANY ATTENTION TO HIM, ROGER.

VIC WILLIAMS AS THE LOBSTER IN *THE PHANTOM JUNGLE* (REPUBLIC, 1945)

THE LOBSTER WAS A FICTIONAL CHARACTER, CREATED IN THE PULP MAGAZINES, MADE POPULAR *BRIEFLY* BY A COUPLE PARTICULARLY BAD MOVIE SERIALS.

*THE VERNAL EQUINOX

SO YOU ARE... WHAT? HOMUNCULUS?

CALL ME ROGER, PLEASE.

WHAT'S UP, BOSS?

HOW DO YOU THINK ROGER'S DOING?

I THINK HE'S DOING GREAT.

I AGREE.

HE'S ADJUSTING BETTER, MUCH *FASTER*, THAN ANYONE EXPECTED. HE'S ADAPTING TO TWENTY-FIRST CENTURY IDEAS AND TECHNOLOGY...

CUTE COUPLE.

SOMETIMES IT'S LIKE WORKING FOR THE GODDAMN CIRCUS.

BUT...?

YOU KNOW THAT ABE BURNED OUT THE SCIENCE LAB SHOCKING ROGER BACK TO LIFE.* YOU KNOW THAT HIS POWER BEGAN TO FADE AGAIN ALMOST IMMEDIATELY...

*ABE SAPIEN VERSUS SCIENCE

" BUT HOW MANY LIVES DID HE *SAVE*, INCLUDING MINE, WHEN HE MELTED HIS BROTHER, THE GIANT HUMAN-FAT MONSTER?

" THEN DIDN'T HE *VOLUNTARILY* ZAP LIZ BACK TO LIFE--

"-- AT THE COST OF HIS *OWN* LIFE?"*

I'M SICK ABOUT WHAT HAPPENED TO BUD, SO IS ROGER, I KNOW IT. BUT THIS SORT OF THING *HAPPENS* IN THIS LINE OF WORK.

LIZ SHERMAN IS ONE OF MY BEST FRIENDS...

...BUT WHEN SHE WAS ELEVEN YEARS OLD SHE BURNED THIRTY-TWO PEOPLE TO DEATH...

WHEN ARE YOU GOING TO PUT A BOMB ON *HER?*

DON'T BE RIDICULOUS. LIZ SHERMAN IS HUMAN, ROGER IS NOT.

I DON'T LIKE THIS ANY MORE THAN YOU DO. I'M JUST TELLING YOU WHAT *I'VE* BEEN TOLD -- ROGER CAN NOT BE ALLOWED TO JEOPARDIZE OTHER AGENTS. HE IS CONSIDERED EXPENDABLE.

TAKE THIS.

WHAT IS IT?

* *HELLBOY: ALMOST COLOSSUS*

...THE SCENIC SOLITUDE! *

SO TELL ME, DO ALL AUSTRIAN SECRET POLICE DOUBLE AS TOUR GUIDES?

NO...

THIS HAS NOTHING TO DO WITH POLICE.

A TERRIBLE SHAPE-CHANGING GIANT, SOMETIMES A WOODCUTTER, SOMETIMES A DONKEY. HE COULD CAUSE SNOW-STORMS AND MAKE LITTLE GIRLS GROW BEARDS.

WE THOUGHT THE CASTLE WAS HIS SO WE WERE AFRAID OF IT.

MY BROTHER WAS A GIANT.

I WAS BORN IN A LITTLE VILLAGE NEAR HERE.

ALL THE CHILDREN USED TO CLIMB IN THESE MOUNTAINS.

SO YOU'VE BEEN UP TO THE CASTLE?

WHEN I WAS LITTLE.

THE OTHERS WOULDN'T GO THERE BE-CAUSE OF THE RÜBEZAHL.

RÜBE-WHO?

LAURA, YOU WERE AFRAID, BUT YOU DID GO TO THE CASTLE, RIGHT?

* FROM "LIGEIA"

I WENT TO PROVE I WAS THE BRAVEST, OF COURSE.

DID YOU GO INSIDE?

ONLY ONCE, AND ONLY A LITTLE WAY...

I WASN'T *THAT* BRAVE.

AND IT WAS DIFFICULT TO FIND A WAY IN BECAUSE OF THE DAMAGE, BUT I--

WAIT.

YOU *THERE!* COME OUT WHERE I CAN SEE YOU!

WHO ARE YOU?

WHAT DO YOU WANT?

TURN BACK.

RÜBEZAHL?

?

ZZZZZZZ--

CHAPTER TWO

* HELLBOY: WAKE THE DEVIL

NO TIME FOR THAT.

YOU SEEM FAMILIAR... MAYBE YOUR VOICE... *SOMETHING*.

I WAS THERE THAT NIGHT WHEN YOU CAME INTO THIS WORLD...

"I WAS POSING AS A SOLDIER THEN, BUT REALLY I WAS AN ASSASSIN COME TO KILL YOU. I KNEW YOU WERE COMING, WHAT YOU WERE...

"ANUNG UN RAMA, THE DESTROYER...

"BUT THAT NIGHT I SAW SOMETHING ELSE IN YOU..."

FREE WILL.

THE CHANCE THAT YOU MIGHT BREAK THE BOUNDS OF FATE AND CHOOSE A LIFE...

"SO I BROKE WITH MY MASTERS AND LET YOU LIVE. TEN YEARS LATER I WATCHED LILLIES GROW OUT OF YOUR SPILLED BLOOD IN SAINT LEONARD'S WOOD* AND I KNEW I HAD DONE THE RIGHT THING."

* HELLBOY: THE NATURE OF THE BEAST

"...AND A MAN WAS SENT TO BE A HOST BODY, A VESSEL--"

POSSESSION BY SPACE-GHOSTS? I DON'T BUY IT.

THE AMERICANS AND RUSSIANS HAVE BEEN SENDING GUYS UP THERE FOR YEARS.

LIVING MEN...

"BUT THE NAZIS SENT A DEAD MAN, AN *EMPTY* VESSEL. HIS BODY WAS SPECIALLY PREPARED FOR THIS PURPOSE...

"...SENT AS A BAITED TRAP INTO A SEA OF MONSTERS...

"NOW, SIXTY-ONE YEARS LATER, SOMEONE HAS RECALLED THE TRAP AND IT'S *DOOM* FOR MAN...

YOU HAVE ENCOUNTERED THE SPECIES BEFORE, IN THE ABBEY OF LA NOE, AND LATER IN THE SEANCE ROOM OF MISTER TOD... *

I SURE AS HELL REMEMBER THAT.

THIS THING THAT'S COMING IS FAR, FAR WORSE. I CAME HERE TO STOP IT, BUT YOU WILL HAVE TO DO IT FOR ME.

I CAN HANDLE IT.

MORE THAN BRUTE FORCE AND BURNING HERBS WILL BE NEEDED. HERE IS A TRAP FROM WHICH THERE IS NO ESCAPE. USE IT.

AH... MY TIME IS NEARLY RUN OUT...

* *HELLBOY: GOODBYE MISTER TOD*

CHAPTER THREE

"WHEN ALL IS DONE, THE WORM WILL TOWER OVER THE WASTE-LAND HE HAS MADE ..."

"HE WILL CALL OUT TO THE STARS THAT *THE THING IS ACCOMPLISHED.* AND THAT, FINALLY, WILL MAKE THE PASSING OF MAN ..."

AMAGOG RAMM JAHURR

"WHEN ALL IS DONE, THE WORM WILL TOWER OVER THE WASTE-LAND HE HAS MADE ...

"HE WILL CALL OUT TO THE STARS THAT *THE THING IS ACCOMPLISHED.* AND THAT, FINALLY, WILL MAKE THE PASSING OF MAN ... "

AMAGOG RAMM JAHURR

"THEN THE THREE HUNDRED AND SIXTY-NINE CHILDREN OF THE OGDRU JAHAD WILL WAKE AND COME UP OUT OF THEIR PRISONS IN THE EARTH AND IN THE SEA.

"THEN THE OGDRU JAHAD WILL WAKE. THE SEVEN WHO ARE ONE, THE SERPENT...

"THEY WILL CAST OFF THEIR CHAINS, COME OUT OF THEIR PRISONS, AND BURN THE EARTH...

"MAKE OF IT A BLACKENED CINDER...

"AND THAT WILL BE THE END.

CHAPTER FOUR

CHAPTER FOUR

HUNTE
CASTLE.
12:18 A.M.

THUD

MIMES, IN THE FORM OF GOD
ON HIGH,
MUTTER AND MUMBLE LOW,
AND HITHER AND THITHER FLY--
MERE PUPPETS THEY, WHO
COME AND GO
AT BIDDING OF VAST FORMLESS
THINGS
THAT SHIFT THE SCENERY
TO AND FRO ...

FLAPPING FROM OUT THEIR
CONDOR WINGS ...

... INVISIBLE WOE!*

* FROM "LIGEIA"

HELLBOY...

" I KNEW HIM FOR WHAT HE WAS AND TRIED TO WAKE HIM TO HIS PURPOSE. WE FOUGHT AND HE DESTROYED ME..."

BUT PART OF ME STILL LIVED IN THE VAMPIRE.

GIURESCU?

JUST AS YOU GAVE ONE HALF OF YOUR SPIRIT TO THE BABA YAGA TO HIDE IN THE ROOTS OF THE WORLD TREE, SO I GAVE A PIECE OF MYSELF TO HIM...

" GIVING HIM THAT NEW LIFE, MAKING HIM MY SON...

" THEN I GAVE HIM UP TO ENTER INTO YOUR FLESH AND IRON MONSTER... *"

AND THE THING NOW IS ME. AS SUCH I WILL GO ON UNTIL THE END OF THE WORLD... AND MAYBE BEYOND THAT.

HE CANNOT. WE ARE BOUND TOGETHER, HE AND I...

HELLBOY DESTROYED YOU ONCE, HE'LL DO IT AGAIN.

* HELLBOY: WAKE THE DEVIL

HELLBOY ™

SKETCHBOOK

The Conqueror Worm himself.
Actually, worms aren't very interesting
looking, so this is based on a caterpillar.

Silver w/ gold swastika

Gold Braid

orange collar tips

Brown Holster & Belt

Inger von Klempt. I tried to avoid the stereotypical skin-tight, black leather, comic-book Nazi superwoman look.

Herman von Klempt, his head jar, and robot body.

Nazi designs:
Human and reptile.

Black Hat &
Collar
w/ Red Design

red

LIGHT BROWN
Shirt & tie

Black
Pants –
Dark
Brown
Belt

Study for Doctor Oeming in
his space capsule. I added a
mustache to avoid confusion
with Lobster Johnson.

Studies for the American soldiers.

The "torture harness" (above) and its control box
(below) which was based on the parking meter
outside my apartment.

And finally the
poor dead alien in
all his glory.

There you go.

MIKE MIGNOLA

Mike Mignola
New York City

HELLBOY

by MIKE MIGNOLA

SEED OF DESTRUCTION
with John Byrne
128-page color paperback
ISBN: 1-56971-316-2 $17.95

WAKE THE DEVIL
144-page color paperback
ISBN: 1-56971-226-3 $17.95

**THE CHAINED COFFIN
AND OTHERS**
168-page color paperback
ISBN: 1-56971-349-9 $17.95

THE RIGHT HAND OF DOOM
144-page color paperback
ISBN: 1-56971-489-4 $17.95

CONQUEROR WORM
144-page color paperback
ISBN: 1-56971-699-4 $17.95

THE LOST ARMY
Written by Christopher Golden
Illustrated by Mike Mignola
208-page B&W paperback
ISBN: 1-56971-185-2 $14.95

ODD JOBS
Short-story collection
with stories by Mike Mignola,
Poppy Z. Brite, Christopher
Golden, and others
Illustrated by Mike Mignola
216-page B&W paperback
ISBN: 1-56971-440-1 $14.95

THE BONES OF GIANTS
Written by Christopher Golden
Illustrated by Mike Mignola
208-page B&W paperback
ISBN: 1-56971-610-2 $14.95

HELLBOY BASEBALL CAP
#17-106 $14.95

HELLBOY SHOT GLASS
Red-and-black Hellboy logo
#17-605 $5.95

HELLBOY LITHOGRAPH
22" x 30" limited edition
#18-029 $100.00

HELLBOY PATCH
3"x 3" embroidered BPRD logo
#17-118 $3.95

**HELLBOY LIMITED-
EDITION WATCH**
Citizen analog quartz watch
packaged in a black matte
wood box with certificate
of authenticity
#17-115 $49.95

**HELLBOY
LUNCH BOX (& POSTCARD)**
Tin de-bossed full-color
#19-012 $19.95

HELLBOY VINYL STATUE
#10-196 $59.99

HELLBOY PVC SET
#10-666 39.99

**HELLBOY
ZIPPO LIGHTER**
#17-101 $29.95

ALSO AVAILABLE
ZOMBIEWORLD
CHAMPION
OF THE WORMS
Mike Mignola & Pat McEown
80-page color paperback
ISBN: 1-56971-334-0 $8.95

HELLBOY BOOKS
AND MERCHANDISE CAN
BE VIEWED AT
www.darkhorse.com

DARK HORSE MAVERICK